celtic
word craft

celtic
word craft

An Introduction to
Welsh Poetic Art

D. IDWAL LLOYD

Dyllansow Truran
Cornish Publications

First published 1985 by Dyllansow Truran, Trewolsta, Trewirgie, Redruth, Cornwall

Designed and typeset by Allset Composition, London
Printed in Great Britain by Penwell, Parkwood, Callington, Kernow, Cornwall
ISBN 1 85022 008 5

contents

ꜰORꜵWORꝆ

Knowing that I am a member of the 'Gorsedd of Bards' in Wales, many many English friends have enquired in which way Welsh poetry differs from that of England. Since it would take a long time to explain orally without teaching aids, I made up my mind to find some publication in English that could enlighten them. Despite much seeking, no such publication was found, so I decided to try and explain the consonance in Welsh poetry as simply as I could, and in such a way that the ordinary reader could understand and appreciate the wordcraft involved. That is how this booklet came about and I hope it will fulfil its purpose.

I am indebted to the following friends for their encouragement and help during the preparation of this work: Mrs Rita Williams, M.A., for valuable suggestions, Mr Walford Parry Jones, B.A., for editing the first draft, Mrs Awena Devonald for typing the manuscript, Dyllansow Truran's reader and proprietor for their confidence in undertaking its publication and Penwell for their usual attractive craftsmanship.

D Idwal Lloyd

pROLOGUe

Prior to being annexed to England by the 1535 Act of Union, Wales had a long cultural tradition. In the area of literature the earliest compositions belong not only to the land today known as Wales, but to Northern England, Southern Scotland and the South West of Britain comprising Cornwall and parts of Devon. These areas and the rest of these Islands were occupied by the Britons before the Angles, Jutes and Saxons settled in the Thames estuary and extended their conquests westwards and northwards. By the year 615AD they had driven a wedge between the peoples of the North and those of Wales. As some of the events that led up to this separation are described in the poems of Aneirin, Morfran, Myrddin and Meugan, the earliest recorded Welsh literature can be said to date from the sixth century. In the poems of the period are descriptions of the exploits of Urien and his cousin Llywarch the Old who were chieftains of the northern territories. These poems seem to have been created ('sung' is the native term) following certain patterns which developed centuries later into a unique consonance or a harmony of sounds and a balance of consonants called 'cynghanedd' – pronounced kung-hah-neth (the final 'th' being sounded as in *th*ee or *th*ou.

The Celts or Britons seem to have been very sound conscious. Their relatives who settled along the Donau, loved pure sound, if we can give that definition to music. Those who moved westwards across Europe on to Britain took a keener interest in the sounds of words although they were not averse to music, for Geraldus Cambrensis, in his record of his itineraries, reports that, whereas the peoples of the part of Britain inhabited by the

ix

English sang in unison, those of Wales sang with four voices. Till this day their ingenuity with words excels their musical creativity.

We are told that one of the wonders of the literature of Wales and of Ireland is the artistic use of words so early in their histories. This applies to prose as well as poetry. To most nations prose was, at first, simply a vehicle for transferring knowledge, preaching or recording history. Its development as an instrument of literature in the short story, novel or essay came much later.

The Celtic interest in words and their sounds led to the development of the consonance mentioned above, and the people who formulated the system were the poets attached to the courts of the princes and the manors of the nobles.

Poets had an honoured place in the homes of the gentry for being the chroniclers of events and the creators of the entertainment, they were an essential part of the household. In social standing they resembled the musicians retained in the regal courts of Europe, so they can undoubtedly be regarded as being professional.

The poet's principal duties were to record and recall events, laud his master's generosity, bravery and wisdom, and praise the virtues, charm and grace of the lady of the house and her offspring. To attain such a position called for much preparation and training. Candidates for the vacancies were believed to be the sons of the upper classes. Whether or not that is correct, it has to be conceded that they must have been young men of much intelligence with an aptitude and ambition to aspire to such a respected position, for it meant a seven to nine year period of preparation. Aspirants were initially classed as 'disgybl ysbas' or learners, progressing by three further stages to qualify as 'pencerdd' or chief poet upon successfully completing the course. The course consisted of theory and practice and progress was by stages of proficiency in language, history, word manipulation and the mastering of the numerous metres. The trainees had also to be able to construct a harp, play all the national airs, set their poems to music and perform before an audience. The setting of the poems to music differed from the generally accepted practice inasmuch as the vocal score was a counter melody to the accompaniment. This practice has survived to the present day in 'penillion' singing, which can often be heard in concerts and eisteddfod competitions in Wales.

Strict rules governed the poetic craft, for the subjects on which the lower grades of performers were allowed to 'sing' were limited and well defined, and even the bards seem to have restricted their compositions to recording historical events, attempts at prophecy, satire, eulogies and elegies. There seem to be few examples of religious compositions among the works of the early poets.

Welsh poets were sponsored or retained by the princes and nobles until the days of Henry VII, when many of them who had helped him to the throne of England were rewarded with the seats and estates of the deposed English nobles. In return, when Henry VIII ascended the throne and decreed that the Welsh language was to be 'extirpated', they were commanded to renounce their mother tongue and adopt that of England. Thus the vacancies for the professional Welsh poets no longer existed, and they had to seek other means of making a living. In spite of this the old Celtic poetic tradition was not annihilated. That it survived is truly amazing considering that the facilities for academic training were practically non-existent. Learning had been more or less confined to the monasteries which were soon dissolved after 1536, leaving Wales with no means of education, other than the church or interested individuals.

Not only did the old poetic tradition overcome what could have been a mortal blow, but it seems to have extended its appeal to people of all classes. It was nursed by interested enthusiasts in all ranks of society, not for any material gains, for there were no financial rewards. It was simply a case of 'old traditions die hard'.

Welsh poetry has been traditionally oral, so its sound was as important as its sense. It had to be aurally pleasing so that the listener could enjoy it even though he or she did not understand every word. Since printing has replaced the laborious copying of manuscripts, books of verse have been readily available so that the appreciation of the poems has been increasingly influenced by the eye more than the ear. As the eye is the gateway to reason, poetry today is more often judged on its logical content, while the patterns of words, metres, rhythm and rhymes are regarded as an additional though not essential ornament. In the past, Welsh poetry was listened to rather than read, hence the importance of its sound to the ear, for the ear is the way to the heart as well as the mind.

Sound, to a musically inclined people, was also an aid to memorisation and so consonance enhanced the former and assisted the latter. Some English critics have dismissed 'cynghanedd' as being 'mere alliteration', but it is far more highly developed than alliteration in any language, as the reader may learn from the simple attempt that follows to explain the intricacies of an art that is an integral part of Welsh poesy.

one

rhythm

Regular rhythm and rhyme were long considered as the primary elements of poetry. Rhythms can be said to be regular patterns of stressed or accented syllables alternating with unstressed or unaccented ones. Words are made up of one or more syllables, for example:

/	/	/	/	/	/
boy	girl	men	feet	great	well

are all single syllable words, which, when alone, are stressed or accented. These are also known as *monosyllabic* words. Where a word is of two syllables it is termed *di-syllabic* and the accent usually falls on the penultimate one, e.g.:

/ —	/ —	/ —	/ —
light-house	post-man	sail-or	high-way.

There are, however, a number of disyllabic words where the accent falls on the final syllable as in:

— /	— /	— /	— /
re-port	un-do	re-call	in-stil.

Where words have three or more syllables they are called *polysyllabic* and in English, the accent in these does not fall regularly on a particular syllable, but varies, as in:

— / —	/ — —	/ — / —	— / — —
recording	musical	revelation	exemplary.

In words of more than three syllables the accent falls on the particular syllable stressed by the speaker in conversation. One

1

person may say the word *continental* stressing the *ent* giving a pattern of:

$$- \quad - \quad / \quad -$$

con-tin-ent-al

while a Welshman's tendency would be to pronounce it with a pattern of:

$$/ \quad - \quad / \quad -$$

con-tin-ent-al.

The difference here can be explained by the fact that the Welshman's natural habit is to emphasise the penultimate syllable in polysyllabic words, as in his own language.

When we put a number of words together we can have either a regular or irregular pattern, i.e. a regular or irregular rhythm. The lines

'God moves in a mysterious way His wonders to perform'

give a pattern thus:

$$- \ / \ - \ / \ - \ / \ - \ / \ - \ / \ - \ / \ - \ /$$

which can be said to be regular. On the other hand

'Have mercy upon me O Lord, for I am weak'

will give a pattern of

$$- \ / \ - \ - \ / \ - \ - \ / \ - \ / \ - \ /$$

which can be seen to be irregular.

As far as can be ascertained, the earliest poems were constructed to a regular rhythm, the rhythm of man's natural movements such as walking, or the rhythms of a trotting or galloping horse. The very earliest rhythm used was probably that of a person walking, a rhythm emphasised by the R.S.M. with his

'Left — Right — Left — Right', with the 'Left' stressed, giving a pattern of:

$$/ - / -.$$

That pattern can be heard in

'Jack and Jill went up the hill to fetch a pail of water'

which can be represented as:

$$/ - / - / - / - / - / - / -.$$

A variation of this rhythm shows the pattern reversed to:

$$- / - / - / - / - / - / - /$$

which is the rhythm found in the well-known hymn, 'O God, our help in ages past . . .'.

Another rhythm from the everyday world around our ancestors was that of the galloping horse:

$$- / - - / - - / - - /.$$

It was this rhythm that made the journey 'From Ghent to Aix' so lively, interesting and real to me as a child when I read the poem.

Those are some of the rhythms found in early poems, and they usually formed a regular pattern to create a verse, with the same pattern repeated for every succeeding verse. There are, of course, the odd exceptions where we get an irregular pattern to a verse, as in some nursery rhymes.

Today, in our highly technological age, the rhythms of everyday life have changed. Fewer people walk and the horse trot and gallop are unfamiliar to the majority. Present-day rhythms are those of mechanical transport and industrial machinery, very often unsynchronised and irregular. That may explain the modern poets' attraction to 'vers libre' or free verse to present their thoughts. Free verse is not as free as the name suggests, for the rhythms are less regular, and to some, more complicated. An examination of the following may prove the point:

> Do not go gentle into that good night,
> Old age should burn and rave at close of day;
> Rage, rage against the dying of the light.

or:

> The force that through the green fuse drives the flower
> Drives my green age.
>
> (both by Dylan Thomas)

Enthusiasts for 'vers libre' maintain that the poet should not be fettered by rules and regulations but given the freedom to express himself unhindered by metre and rhyme.

two
Rhyme

Rhyme is an identity of sound between words, extending from the end to the last fully accented syllable, eg:

'greet – deceit'; 'shepherd – leopard'; 'quality – frivolity'

are regarded as being perfect rhymes in English, whereas 'seat' and 'deceit'; 'station' and 'crustacean' would not. 'Love' as a rhyme to 'move' or 'prove' is allowed in English although they are classed as imperfect rhymes. To a Welsh poet, the words would in no way be considered as rhyming. Neither would 'come' and 'home' as found in 'Our God, our help in ages past', nor 'die' and 'eternity' as seen in the last verse of the hymn, 'Breathe on me, breath of God'.

The Welsh poet's ear would demand words such as 'roam', 'loam' or 'dome' to rhyme with 'home' and would totally reject 'come' and 'some'. Yet, when it comes to disyllabic or poly-syllabic words, the Welsh poet's ear seems less sensitive than that of his neighbour. The Welsh, when writing in English, will rhyme 'writing' with 'reading', or 'nation' with 'caution' for the first pair end with the same 'ing' sound, and the second pair have the 'shun' sound in common. English poets would require words like 'elation', 'station', 'relation' or 'creation' to rhyme with 'nation'; and 'fighting', 'lighting', 'whiting' or 'exciting' to rhyme with 'writing'. They would never consider rhyming an accented word with an unaccented one, but in Welsh poetry it is common practice. In the couplet

'Night may dare / not my dearest
Shadow / throw / where she doth rest'

5

the words 'rest' and 'dearest' are accepted rhymes, or rhymes that are deemed correct. Similarly 'death' and 'restoreth' or 'abideth' are considered as correct. This practice of rhyming an accented with an unaccented syllable probably came about between the tenth and twelfth centuries, when the accent, which up till then had been on the final or ultimate syllable, was moved to the penultimate. That this actually happened is a recognised fact among the language experts, but the reason for the change remains obscure.

When Welsh poets use rhymes similar to their English counter-parts, with polysyllabic words like 'nation' and 'inflation' or 'station', they call them 'double rhymes' and often use these terminally and internally for harmonic effect.

three

harmony: the poet's craft

The *Echoing Harmony*

The Welsh poet's craft is called 'cynghanedd', as explained in the prologue. The word could be translated as *harmony*, for it is the melodious effect produced by the use of rhyme and corresponding patterns of consonants, or a combination of both.

There are four types of harmony used, one using a kind of internal rhyme only, two involving the use of consonantal balance and the fourth using both rhyme and a balance of consonants. The simplest of the four, which uses rhyme only, is the 'cynghanedd lusg' or 'drawn harmony'. For ease of understanding we will call it the *echoing harmony*. It can only occur in lines which end in a polysyllabic word where the accent falls on the last syllable but one, which we will henceforth call the penultimate syllable, e.g.: in words like

        end-ing   plac-es   phon-et-ic   un-der-stand-ing
         /   —   /   —   — / —   —   —   /   —

but not

        re-peat   ech-o-ing   Jan-u-ary   in-dir-ect
         —   /   / — —   / — —   —   —   /

To form the *echoing harmony* you need an accented word, or a word whose final syllable is stressed, near the natural rest in the line (called the caesura), which rhymes with the penultimate syllable that is also accented, e.g.:

> The b*end* was never-*end*ing

or

> It was a gr*and* underst*and*ing

7

and

The word 'b*et*' is phon*et*ic.

If these lines are read aloud, the echo of the words *bend, grand* and *bet* can be heard in the penultimate syllables of the words *ending, understanding* and *phonetic.*

When the mid-line accented word rhyming with the penultimate syllable comes very early in the line the echo is not so evident, so the line is not considered a strong one.

'The crowd I was told was rowdy'

is quite correct, but the echo is not as audible in

'I'm told the crowd was rowdy'.

It is advisable to try the line orally to find the place for the mid-line accented word and then choose the one that sounds best.

Trying the line orally means using the ear, rather than the eye. Appreciation to many today depends on the eye and the intellect, but with 'Cynghanedd' the eye can deceive more often than the ear, e.g.:

'Ten gross? Now that's colossal!'

This looks right, but when read aloud it will be noticed that the vowel *o* in *gross* is longer or heavier than the *o* in *colossal*, so there is actually no echo, and the harmony is broken. On the other hand, the line

'She has the guile of Delilah'

looks wrong to the eye but is correct to the ear, which of course, it is. The same can be said of

'I found peace by the seaside'

which may appear wrong visually but is aurally correct.
A less sensitive ear could be deceived by

> 'He ran down the gangway'

but as *ran* and *gang* do not rhyme there is no echo, and the line must be regarded as deficient or incorrect. It would be correct if changed to

> 'His voice rang from the gangway'.

In Welsh the mid-line word rhyming with the penultimate syllable can be polysyllabic, e.g.:

> 'Dyma ard*al* fy ngh*al*on'

(literally, 'this is the district of my heart' or 'this is the region I love).

Owing to the English rhyming rules this is not possible unless:

> He kept abus*ing* the w*ing*er

or

> He is the ag*ent* for all the c*ent*res

can be accepted.

Here are a number of examples for you to read aloud and analyse:

> He must be dense or senseless!
> At night the Count crossed the mountains.
> I met a guard from Cardiff.
> 'Twas ten degrees below freezing.
> I was born in the morning.
> 'Seven knots', said the yachtsman.
> His Grace was at the races.

Some sounds at night are fright'ning.
I sent the bitch to Richmond.
I found myself in Belfast!
What a disgrace he faces!
They closed the fund on Monday.

* * *

Lines containing this type of *echoing harmony* can be found in the works of Icelandic poets of the Middle Ages, probably the only examples yet discovered outside the old Celtic culture.

The *'Criss-Cross' Harmony*

If the 'echoing harmony' is regarded as the simplest of the four types used by Welsh poets, the 'cynghanedd groes' or the 'criss-cross' harmony is the most intricate. Here the aim, or art, is to balance the consonants in the two halves of the line on either side of the caesura. Take the line:

'I love a green olive grove'.

The natural break, rest, or caesura, comes after the word *green*:

'I love a green / olive grove'.

Now when we reduce the line to the bare sounded consonants, (consonants that have no sound, known as 'silent letters', are entirely ignored, for they cannot affect the sound), we get:

$$ l \ v \ g \ r \ ^\backslash \ n \ / \ l \ v \ g \ r \ ^\backslash \ v. $$

The consonants in both parts of the line are identical and in the same order *apart from* the ones after the accent in 'green' and 'grove'. If these, too, were identical the line would lose much of its music. When we compare:

'I love a green olive grove'

with

'One lonely grave in a lonely grove'

the ear seems to dislike, if not object to, 'grave' — 'grove', and prefers the 'green' — 'grove' combination as being more pleasant aurally. The same is true of:

'In a house on a hill'

and

'In a hall on a hill'.

The examples given above have accented words at the end of both parts of the line. The same is true of these:

'You pin the bill / upon the board'
p n th b\l   p n th b \rd

'Willie lives / all alone'
l   l v\s / l l\n

and

'All the boys will thee obey'
l th b\ s / l th   b\

Next let us consider lines where the syllable immediately before the caesura is accented, while the final syllable in the line is unaccented. When this occurs then the final consonant of the mid-line accented syllable has to be echoed. Take the example:

'Can't the men / count the money?'
c nt th m\n / c   nt th m\n ͜

The 'n' in the word 'men' next to the caesura has to be answered or echoed in the final disyllabic word 'money' before the harmony is aurally complete. The ear would not hear any harmony if the line ran thus:

> 'Can't the men count the motors?'

for the word 'motors' seems discordant. Similarly:

> 'Veda might / have conceded'

does not convey a sense of harmony to the ear as would be the case if it were changed to:

> 'Veda might / have admitted'.

The same is true of:

> 'Sue is afraid, so is Kathleen'

when compared with:

> 'Sue is afraid, so is Freda'.

When the words next before the caesura and the final word are disyllabic or polysyllabic, all the consonants, except the ones that end those words have to be answered. The following examples will help to elucidate the points:

> 'Love beckoned Olive Baker'
> l v b \ k ⌣ *nd* / l v b\k⌣*r*

The word next to the caesura and the last in the line are disyllabic with the accent on the first syllable in both, so that the vowels between the 'b' and 'k' are stressed and the syllable after the 'k' sound in both is unaccented. All the consonants, including the ones stressed are echoed, but the final consonants in 'beckoned' and 'Baker' are not. The 'nd' sound at the end of 'beckoned' differs from the 'r' ending the word 'Baker'. If both of these were alike the harmony would suffer, e.g.:

'Love beckoned Olive Bacon'

is not as sonorous as the previous line, as it seems more like a repeated note than a harmony. For the same reason, the ear would rather hear:

'For I'm British, from Brighton'

than:

'For I'm a Briton from Brighton'.

It sometimes happens that the word ending one of the parts of the line terminates in a consonant while the other ends in a vowel or dipthong. This is always acceptable as long as the endings of both words are different, otherwise you get an effect that is not so aurally pleasing. Lines, such as:

'Nor a volley in our valley'

or

'Roy Bailey, you're a bully!'

have similar endings that are not as acceptable to the ear as:

'Near a village in our valley'

or

'Roy Bailey, you are bawling!'

Here are two more examples with a vowel or dipthong ending one of the two parts of a line:

'Free Melinda from London'

and

'Go tomorrow, get married'.

In the *criss-cross harmony*, where the words that end both
parts of a line are balanced, i.e. both being monosyllabic, or both
polysyllabic and similarly accented, then the two parts can be
reversed or interchanged, e.g.:

'Go tomorrow, get married'

can be changed thus:

'Get married, Go tomorrow'.

Both lines, when analysed, can be seen to conform to the rules
stated above. The same is true of:

'As with the soul so they sing'

So they sing as with the soul'

and also

I fain would do a fine deed'

A fine deed I fain would do'

The *criss-cross harmony* is sometimes further complicated into
a *linked criss-cross harmony*, where to get the balance of consonants, the two halves of the line have to be linked across the
caesura, e.g.:

Solly lives / all alone'
s l l\v s   l l \n

It will be noticed that the consonants in the first half of the line are *s l l* whereas those in the second half are just the two *l's*. To get the *s* needed to balance both parts, we have to overlap or link the two halves thus:

'Solly lives all alone'
s l   l\v⑤ l l\n

and

'Dannie landed / in London'
d n   l\ndd/ n l \nd⌣n

By the linking, or overlapping, the line would sound as if it were written:

'Dannie lande / din London'

and when analysed shows the balance of consonants called for.

Mastery of this type of harmony comes from experience and a good vocabulary! Still, lines containing this particular harmony are not uncommon in the work of Welsh poets of all classes.

Here are a few more examples of the *criss-cross harmony* to study and analyse:

'I shan't applaud ancient plants'
'His writing is so rotten'
'A wild growling old gorilla'
'Tilly wrote to Lorretta'
'Levi will date a lovely doll'
'Does my period seem poorer?'<br>'Maisie seldom saw a soldier'
'One frame I brought now from Brighton'
'Don't you ride into Reading'
'As benign as bananas'
'Pin the bill upon the board'.

The *Bridging Harmony*
If you have grasped the underlying principles of the *criss-cross*
harmony then the remaining types should present no difficulty
for they are easier to follow and construct. The third type is
called 'cynghanedd draws', which, literally translated, means
'*trans harmony*', but we shall call it the *bridging harmony*. It is
very similar to the *criss-cross harmony*, but is not as demanding,
as there is an interval or gap containing one or more consonants
in the second half of the line before the echo of the consonants
in the first half of the line is heard. But the echo must be a true
one. Once the gap has been bridged the consonants must appear
in the same unbroken sequence as they do in the first half of the
line. The consonants that appear in the interval or gap need not
be echoed. Take the line:

I am pleased / with my plums.
m pl \ sd /   th *m*   *pl*\ms

The *m, p, l* in the first half of the line are found in the same order
in the second half, but the *th* in *with* goes unechoed so we 'go
over' or *bridge* it. The sounds *sd* at the end of *pleased* and the
ms at the end of *plums* are different so as to avoid any mono-
tony or discord to the ear. The same is true of:

Diana lives / right down a lane.
d   n   l \vs / r   t *d   n   l* \n

There we have the consonants *d, n* and *l* echoed on either side of
the caesura, in the same order, but the *r* and *t* in *right* are not,
and so are *bridged* as are the *n* and *k* in:

Too many dogs / in Katmandu.
t   m n   d \gs / n k *tm   d* \

These are examples where the syllable next before the caesura
and the final syllable are accented.

When the syllable next before the caesura is accented, and the final syllable in the line is unaccented, then the consonant(s) ending the mid-line word must be echoed in the second half of that line, usually after the accent in the last polysyllabic word in the line, e.g.:

Harry drove / with other drivers.
r   dr\v   /   th   th r dr\v ˘

Here the *v* in *drove* has to be echoed after the accent in the final word, as it is in *drivers*. If a word like *drummers* was substituted the line would lose its harmony:

Harry drove with other drummers.

Similarly:

May I ask for some water?

does not strike the ear as being very sonorous, whereas:

May I ask for some whisky?

is at least more interesting aurally!
Other examples of this type are:

My bank / must think I'm bonkers!
Vera Knight / was very naughty.
Are you afraid / for our freedom?
'Tis so bare / that it's boring!
I find I've a mate / who's fond of meetings.

Some lines in the *bridging harmony* as in the *criss-cross harmony* have polysyllabic words ending in an unaccented syllable next before the caesura and at the end. The same rule applies to both, except that in the *bridging harmony* some consonants after the caesura can be left unechoed as explained, for example:

Sue carried / her mascara.

It can be seen that the *r* in *carried* is echoed in *mascara* but the *r* in *her* and the *m* in *mascara* are not echoed but bridged.
In the following example:

You seldom / meet a soldier

the *ld* in *seldom* is echoed in the word *soldier*, and the *m* and *t* in *meet* are bridged. The consonants ending the words *seldom* and *soldier* differ by design as previously explained.

* * *

Here are some more examples of the *bridging harmony* to study and analyse:

'Hot his brow, bated his breath'
'His soul for luck he selleth'
'And the dark creeps round the door'
'Tommorow I get married'
'Gloating o'er heaps that glitter.'
A serious hidden sorrow.
I may marry Sammy Morris!
I hope that you'll be happy.
He worried o'er the warrant.
I mainly go by moonlight.
My parents were imperilled.
Where daylight ever dallies.
I love your part of Liverpool. (with the accent on *pool*)
I knew the tallest there in the twilight.
I have no mind to leave on Monday!
I knew the maiden you met in the meadow.

The *Sonorous Harmony*
The fourth and final harmony is the 'cynghanedd sain' which
could be translated as the harmony of sound, but which we will
call the *sonorous harmony* on account of its pleasing effect. In
this type,the line falls into, not two, but three parts, with the
first and second parts rhyming and the second and third parts
having a repeat pattern of consonants as explained in the *criss-
cross* and *bridging* harmonies. Let us look at the following line:

I saw Jen and Ken in court

which divides itself into these three parts:

I saw Jen / and Ken / in court.

You will notice that the first and second parts have the words
'Jen' and 'Ken', words that rhyme, while the second and third
parts have a balance of the 'k' sound in the words 'Ken' and
'court'. The same pattern can be seen in:

Along the roads / went loads / of lime
l \   l \

where the first two parts rhyme and the second and third parts
have a common consonant 'l' before the accent. These lines obey
the same rules:

We'll walk / and talk / by the Thames.
He is dead / in head / and heart.
We keep / the sheep / in a shed.
They wined / and dined / by the Dee.

Whether the words ending the first and second parts are monosyllabic or polysyllabic they must always rhyme and the rules
explained in the *criss-cross* and *bridging* harmonies apply when
the words ending the second and third parts are accented or
unaccented.

In the second and third parts of a line which has the *sonorous harmony* the balance of consonants can be either full as in the *criss-cross harmony* or partial as in the *bridging harmony* explained above. An analysis of the following will help the reader to comprehend the points made:

His *crime* / meant *time* / for Tommy
t′m   t′m

When we *sail* / don't *fail* / to follow
t f′l   t f′l

Their gar*den* / of E*den* / was invaded
v   ′d˅   v′d˅

'Where ashpho*dels* / and blueb*ells* / blow'
bl \   bl

(G. M. Hopkins)

Further examples to study:

> Eddy was already reading (or riding).
> He was too dense to fence the field!
> I saw my love above the beach.
> Teddy was a steady student.
> He still longs for the songs of the sea.
> Beyond the pass no grass will grow.
> I have a mind to grind old Grundy!
> We'll wine and dine on the Donau.

four
a question
of consonants

In Welsh every consonant has one sound, but there are two consonants that have the same sound, viz: 'ff' and 'ph'. In English a number of consonants have more than one sound, and some, called 'silent letters', no sound at all. As the latter play no part in the harmonies explained in this exposition, they can be ignored, but the former need to be considered.

Where two identically sounding consonants appear side by side, or together, as in 'quiet talk', 'clean napkin' or 'butter', 'pepper' or 'little', they can be answered or balanced by one similar letter as the ear cannot easily separate the two:

'It's a bet that it's butter'

or

'Like his pop he likes pepper'.

Of the consonants with more than one sound, let us first consider the letter 'c', which has no individual sound of its own, but is sounded either as a 'k' or an 's', as is directed by the old rhyme:

'Before an 'u' an 'o' an 'a'
The 'c' is sounded as a 'k';
Before a 'y' an 'i' an 'e'
'Tis like an 's' you sound the 'c'.'

As has been previously stressed, it is the sound and not the appearance that counts, the 'c' must be answered or balanced

21

by a similar sounding 'c', an 's', a 'k' or 'ck', e.g.:

Sir, you sign / as received
s r   s\n / s r s \ d

or:

You recall our account
r c\l / r   c \ nt

And again,

Biddy had a kiddy cart
B*iddy* / had a k*iddy* / cart
k '   / k '

The letter *f* has two sounds associated with it, viz, a *v* sound in the word *of* and the *f* sound as in *off* and *face*. The former will have to be answered by a *v* at all times, while the second can be echoed by itself, *ff, ph* as in *phone* or *gh* as in *laugh*.

The letter *g* is another dual consonant, for it can be balanced by a *g* when sounded as in *get* or *gain*, and by a *j* when sounded as in *gem* or *gesture*.

As has been previously emphasised, all silent letters need not be echoed, but ignored, so that the *h* in *hour* and *honour* need not be considered, but the *h* in *hand* or *heat* should be balanced by a similar aspirate, as in:

He was *dead* / in *head* / and heart
h '   /   h '

When *gh* appears as in *dough, plough* or *though* the symbol has no consonantal sound and should be treated as silent, but when sounded as in *cough, trough, rough* or *laugh* it should be echoed by a similar sounding letter, which could be any one of these — *f* as in *face; ff* as in *off* or *ph* as in *phantom*.

The letter *q* has a *k* sound and should be echoed by any letter or combination of letters giving the same sound, which could be a *k, ck, cc* (as in account) or a *c* representing a *k* sound.

You are right / he's quite / a case
You were right / he's quite / a kid!
He was quick / with his account

The *s* too, is a dual consonant for it has a hard sound as in *safe, socks* or *sailor* and a soft sound as in *lives* or *roses.* The hard sounding *s* will always be echoed by a similar sounding letter like the *c* in *cease*, while the softer one can be echoed by a soft *s* as in *rise* or a *z* as in *lazy.*

The symbol *th* has two sounds, one that can be termed hard as in *thank, thrive* or *throw*, and the second, soft, as in *these, those, thee* or *thou.* These should be balanced hard by hard or soft by soft but never hard by soft or vice versa.

The letter *x* can be echoed by another *x*, by *cks* or *ks* as they have a similar sound.

Rex felt / the loose rocks fall.

Or:

Rex fumed / when the racks fell.

A *z* can be answered by a *z* or by a soft *s* as in *resin* or *rose.*

* * *

Sir Idris Bell's observation on the Welsh alphabet may be of interest to the reader. Sir Idris was an East Anglian who mastered the Welsh language and became a recognised authority on many aspects of it. Comparing the two languages, Welsh and English, he considered the Welsh consonants as being more dramatic than those in the English language and the vowels cleaner. This may explain the attraction of consonance in Welsh poetry and account for its continuance.

ꝼıⱴe

ꝳetꝶeꞅ anꝺ
applıcatıon

Metres or verse forms are found in the literature of all nations, some of them common to many countries. A few, like the sonnet and limerick, can be claimed by a particular area or country. What makes the Welsh metres distinctive is the inclusion of the consonance, and the fact that they were standardised and reduced to twenty-four in number by Dafydd ap Edmwnd in the Carmarthen Eisteddfod of 1451. Today, of those twenty-four, only around a quarter of them are being used. The ones disregarded are the more intricate and longer monorhyming examples which were only used as demanding exercises for the trainee bards. During the later stages of their long course these bards had to compose an ode containing all twenty-four metres! Today, however, the two most used or most popular are the 'cywydd' and the 'englyn'. The 'cywydd' is a poem of indeterminate length consisting of seven syllable couplets ending alternately in accented and unaccented rhyming words, e.g.:

> Night may dare / not my dearest
> Shadow / throw / where she doth rest.

Every line in the 'cywydd' must contain one of the harmonies explained in Chapter 3. Equally popular, if not more so, is the 'englyn' or stanza, which in one way resembles the Greek epigram. It is a form much used for epitaphs, and many, many examples can be seen in headstones in the churchyards in Wales. The 'englyn' is a four line composition of thirty syllables. The first line has ten syllables made up of seven plus three, or eight plus two, with the final word of the seven (or eight as the case may be) rhyming with the endings of the other three lines. The three (or two) syllables that make up the ten syllables in the first line are regarded as a part of the second line of six syllables and have a balance of consonants with the first half of that line. The second part of the second line need not be included in the consonance but it has to end in a polysyllabic word. The third and fourth lines are identical with those of the 'cywydd' and must therefore contain the harmonies listed above, but it is advisable not to use the *echoing harmony* in the last line. An analysis of a lighthearted stanza by Bodfan will help to clarify the somewhat involved explanation:

> I am weary / I am worried, — I feel lost,
> I'm flustered / and flurried;
> I fain would do / a fine deed,
> Tomorrow / I get married.

The first line is of ten syllables, i.e. seven plus three. The seven, as you can see, have a *criss-cross harmony*. The three syllables after the pause in the first line and the early part of the second line, viz: 'I feel lost, I'm flustered' give a *bridging harmony*, as you span the 'm' before flustered. The third line, 'I fain would do a fine deed' is another *criss-cross harmony*, for the 'l' in 'would' is silent and need not be echoed. The last line, 'Tomorrow I get married' is another example of the *briding harmony* as the 'g' in 'get' is not answered. All four lines end in words which, to a Welsh reader, rhyme — 'worried', 'flurried', 'deed' and 'married', and that is because rhyming an accented with an unaccented one is not only acceptable but essential.

* * *

In explaining the intricacies of the 'cynghanedd' it was stated that the phonological characteristics of the language were a contributory factor in its formation and development. This does not mean that the system can only be practised in a nearly purely phonetic language. It should prove easier in such a language, but it should not prove impossible in others. Lamartine, 1790—1869, for instance, has an occasional line in his French poems, and French is not a very phonetic language! (Apparently he learned of the Celtic system through his wife's connection with Wales.)

Poets outside Wales have taken an interest in the poetic system of the Principality and have tried their hand at adorning their own compositions in a similar manner. One of these was William Barnes, born in Dorset in 1800. He spent periods with friends in Wales and took an interest in the consonance which is reflected in his poems, especially the one to Linden Lee where we find the line:

> '. . . . . do
> Lean down low in Linden Lee'.

Thomas Hardy, born near Dorchester in 1840, shows in some of his poems that he was aware of the 'cynghanedd' or consonance. This may not be immediately evident to the reader until he reads the lines aloud. These examples are taken from the 'Lost Pyx':

> 'Some say the spot is banned, that the pillar Cross-in-Hand
> Attests the deeds of Hell'.

Although that line is not as closely woven as some of the examples given earlier, the sonorous harmony can be heard in 'banned', 'hand', 'hell'. The same can be said of:

> 'But else than of bale is the mystic tale
> The ancient Vale folk tell'.

Several critics dealing with the work of Gerard Manley Hopkins, born in Stratford, Essex, in 1844, speak of 'sprung rhythm' and 'complicated internal rhymes', not knowing that these were the result of a conscious attempt to adopt and adapt the Welsh 'cynghanedd' to his English compositions. If this has given rise to the 'sprung rhythm' in English verse then that is a bonus. It could be argued that the line:

'Where ashphodels and bluebells blow'

could have been quite accidental, and not a conscious attempt to construct a line of sonorous harmony, and that such happy accidents do occur in poetry. Even if that argument is put forward it must most certainly be disproved when we find a line like:

'Life is a dance ϕ that ϕ laughs away death'

which is a first class example of the *bridging harmony*, and the result of meditation, inspiration and a knowledge of the Celtic consonance. A study of 'The Wreck of the Deutschland' and his other poems will yield further examples.

The attempts by the above poets indicate that it is possible to compose in 'cynghanedd' in English. Doubtless it should prove easier in more phonetic languages, e.g. German, for lines like these:

'Durch einen wilden Wald'

and

'Was kosst so sanft und kusst so suss'

are found in the work of Uhland, and seem to suggest that he had come in contact with someone familiar with the consonance used by the poets of Wales.

Further examples of the use of 'cynghanedd' by English and other poets can be seen in the writings of Aneurin Talfan Davies, who made a special study of its use by English and Anglo-Welsh writers.

'Cynghanedd' in English by Welsh Poets

Many Welsh-speaking poets have tried their hand at writing verses in English which contain the Celtic cynghanedd. Most of them have taken the 'englyn' as their metre, and usually their attempts are in a lighter vein. Waldo Williams, one of Wales' great poets of this century, took a cottage near Haverfordwest where he resided alone after retiring. One day he heard his sister's English friend enquire whether he was agile and active enough, in his late sixties, to look after himself. His reaction to the question was:

> On my own now I manage, — a repast
> I prepare with courage;
> I live active for my age
> In a cute little cottage.

Stanzas in a more serious mood are not as numerous or well-known. The following, by a minister using the bardic name, Bodfan, is an attempt to describe an inconsiderate person:

> He's a cad, though he's a King, — he's one man
> Who's unmoved by suff'ring;
> He has no fellow feeling
> Nor one thought for any thing.

Eifion Wyn, a Carnarvonshire poet of the first half of this century penned the following to the gambler:

> Gloating o'er heaps that glitter, — at his board
> He sits bent in pleasure;
> He yields to sport's wildest spur,
> Woos luck and covets lucre.

> Hot his brow, bated his breath, — in fool's haunts
> 'Mid foul sin he lurketh;
> His soul for luck he selleth
> And ruined dies a drawn death.

One of the best attempts I have come across is the following tribute to the nurse, written by John Boncath Evans, a schoolmaster at Newchapel, North Pembrokeshire during the early part of this century:

> Kind skill the nurse disburseth — with solace
> Those ailing she cheereth;
> Where doth loom the doom of death
> Obedient she abideth.

A detailed examination of the above stanzas will reveal the use of the harmonies explained in the body of this booklet. It is interesting to note that the one to the nurse has an example of all four types. The echoing harmony in the first line is evident, while the criss-cross harmony can be seen in 'with solace — those ailing', the sonorous harmony in the third line and the bridging harmony in the last, being that the *sh* in *she* is not echoed.

The author, seeking to justify his assertion that it is possible to write a serious 'englyn' or stanza in English, and to satisfy himself, meditated thus on man's folly:

> Anxious for some distinction — we're ever
> Driven by ambition,
> While we know all will anon
> Be levelled in oblivion.

epilocue

Here endeth the attempt to give you a simplified exposition of the vocalic and consonantal harmonies found in Welsh poetry. The examples given, apart from those quoted, have been made as ordinary and prosaic as possible so as not to distract the reader's attention from the form by the content. By so doing, I hope that I have been able to prove to those people who would dismiss the system as 'mere alliteration', that they are well wide of the mark.

Many critics, and some poets, believe that restrictions and constrictions of this type are a severe handicap to the writing of good poetry. They are the exponents of 'vers libre' who demand unfettered freedom. On the other hand, W. H. Auden maintained that metre and rhyme were needed to discipline a poet, an opinion to which many Welsh poets would subscribe. Doubtless, much inferior poetry has been composed in these strict metres by less competent men, whose work is little more than an attempt at an intellectual exercise or dishonest sentimentality. It is equally true to say that many poems that can stand side by side with the world's classics have come from the pens of those inspired poets who had mastered the art and have given us masterpieces filled with sincere sentiments and noble thoughts.

The champions of free verse cannot claim that everything written in that mode is of premier quality, as a great deal of it is of very questionable standard, for its freedom does not ensure excellence.

No one will doubt that too much ingenuity is a mistake, for it is a sure sign of decadence, in any art, to multiply extravagant and useless ornament at the expense of simplicity and symmetry. Yet the masters among Welsh poets through the ages have been

30

able to give us the simplicity and symmetry in this intricate consonance, which seems to have flowed naturally from their environment and inspiration.

Another criticism levelled at the system is that it is far too difficult to master by any person who does not possess a first class honours degree in language. History disproves this assertion, for the premier poetry award in Wales, viz., the chair of the National Eisteddfod, given for the best ode (a poem of 250–300 lines) written in these strict metres, has been won by lesser mortals. Two recent winning odes have been classed by the judges and critics alike as being outstanding contributions to Welsh literature. One was the work of a quarryman, whose formal education (and that to all intents and purposes entirely in English) came to an end in the village elementary school. The other was composed by a young farmer who had had a few years in a secondary school but no college. This proves that though the system may be aristocratic in form it is certainly truly democratic in spirit.

People from all walks of life who practice the art today, are continuing a tradition which has more than a thousand years of unbroken development and usage. The word 'unbroken' is used despite the change in the fortunes of Welsh poets after 1535. Prior to the accession of Henry VIII to the throne of England, the poets of Wales were middle to upper class professionals, but after the removal of their sponsors and the dissolution of the monasteries, their source of education, the art was continued by interested amateurs. These part-timers came from all ranks of society, and they passed on their heritage to succeeding generations of interested individuals. As a result, it is probably true to say that there are more men (and a few women) practising the art today than there were in pre-Tudor times.

It cannot be denied that after the days of the Tudors the general standard deteriorated for some time, as the natural development was arrested, not only by the drastic change, but by the imposition upon the people of alien standards and values. Another factor, frequently forgotten, was that the Act of Union virtually destroyed the cultural links between Wales and the continent of Europe, so that the only standards recognised, until more recent times, were those prevailing beyond Offa's Dyke. During succeeding generations the Welsh were obliged to look at Europe through English eyes, when they were conditioned to believe that Welsh scholarship was of little interest and of less value to anybody, and that the Welsh language was a very severe handicap to all who spoke it. Such conditioning could not but adversely affect the native culture.

Despite the revival of interest in all things Welsh during this century, the effects of that insidious genocidal propaganda, assisted by the overwhelming power of the media, still threaten extinction. That the language and the poetic tradition have so far survived must be one of the marvels of modern times, and while the language lives the old Celtic wordcraft will continue to flourish as a unique feature in world literature.

SOURCES

Cerdd Dafod. Sir John Morris Jones
  Clarendon Press, Oxford, 1925
Welsh Poetic Art. Prof. T. Gwyn Jones, M.A.
  Y Cymrodor (Magazine of Hon. Soc. of Cymrodorion), Devises, Printed
  1926
O Drum i Draeth. Eifion Wyn
  Foyles Welsh Press, London, 1929
Englynion. Bodfan
  Hughes and Son, Wrexham, 1933
Twf y Gynghanedd. Sir Thomas Parry, M.A., D.Lit.
  Cyfres y Brifysgol a'r Werin, Cardiff, 1938
Odl a Chynghanedd. Dewi Emrys James
  Foyles, London, 1938 and 1941
  Llyfrau'r Dryw, Llandybie, 1938
The Development of Welsh Poetry. Sir Idris Bell
  Clarendon Press, Oxford, 1955
Hanes ein Llên. Sir Thomas Parry
  Cyfres y Brifysgol a'r Werin, Cardiff, 1948
Highlights of Welsh Literature. R. M. Jones
  Christopher Davies, Wales, 1971
Anghenion y Gynghanedd. Alan Lloyd Roberts (Alan Llwyd)
  Welsh University Press, Cardiff, 1973

The unpublished manuscripts of the late Mr. Aneurin Talfan Davies may be traced in the Manuscript Department of the National Library of Wales, Aberystwyth.

33